This book belongs to

_____

2022

Garden Planner

2022

January

MON	TUE	WED	THU	FRI	SAT	SUN
					1	2
3	4	5	6	7	8	9
10	11	12	13	14	15	16
17	18	19	20	21	22	23
24	25	26	27	28	29	30
31						

February

MON	TUE	WED	THU	FRI	SAT	SUN
	1	2	3	4	5	6
7	8	9	10	11	12	13
14	15	16	17	18	19	20
21	22	23	24	25	26	27
28						

March

MON	TUE	WED	THU	FRI	SAT	SUN
	1	2	3	4	5	6
7	8	9	10	11	12	13
14	15	16	17	18	19	20
21	22	23	24	25	26	27
28	29	30	31			

April

MON	TUE	WED	THU	FRI	SAT	SUN
				1	2	3
4	5	6	7	8	9	10
11	12	13	14	15	16	17
18	19	20	21	22	23	24
25	26	27	28	29	30	

May

MON	TUE	WED	THU	FRI	SAT	SUN
						1
2	3	4	5	6	7	8
9	10	11	12	13	14	15
16	17	18	19	20	21	22
23	24	25	26	27	28	29
30	31					

June

MON	TUE	WED	THU	FRI	SAT	SUN
	1	2	3	4	5	
6	7	8	9	10	11	12
13	14	15	16	17	18	19
20	21	22	23	24	25	26
27	28	29	30			

July

MON	TUE	WED	THU	FRI	SAT	SUN
				1	2	3
4	5	6	7	8	9	10
11	12	13	14	15	16	17
18	19	20	21	22	23	24
25	26	27	28	29	30	31

August

MON	TUE	WED	THU	FRI	SAT	SUN
1	2	3	4	5	6	7
8	9	10	11	12	13	14
15	16	17	18	19	20	21
22	23	24	25	26	27	28
29	30	31				

September

MON	TUE	WED	THU	FRI	SAT	SUN
			1	2	3	4
5	6	7	8	9	10	11
12	13	14	15	16	17	18
19	20	21	22	23	24	25
26	27	28	29	30		

October

MON	TUE	WED	THU	FRI	SAT	SUN
					1	2
3	4	5	6	7	8	9
10	11	12	13	14	15	16
17	18	19	20	21	22	23
24	25	26	27	28	29	30
31						

November

MON	TUE	WED	THU	FRI	SAT	SUN
	1	2	3	4	5	6
7	8	9	10	11	12	13
14	15	16	17	18	19	20
21	22	23	24	25	26	27
28	29	30				

December

MON	TUE	WED	THU	FRI	SAT	SUN
			1	2	3	4
5	6	7	8	9	10	11
12	13	14	15	16	17	18
19	20	21	22	23	24	25
26	27	28	29	30	31	

🍃 Wish List 🍃

Wish List

2022

January

MON	TUE	WED	THU	FRI	SAT	SUN
					1	2
3	4	5	6	7	8	9
10	11	12	13	14	15	16
17	18	19	20	21	22	23
24	25	26	27	28	29	30
31						

February

MON	TUE	WED	THU	FRI	SAT	SUN
	1	2	3	4	5	6
7	8	9	10	11	12	13
14	15	16	17	18	19	20
21	22	23	24	25	26	27
28						

March

MON	TUE	WED	THU	FRI	SAT	SUN
	1	2	3	4	5	6
7	8	9	10	11	12	13
14	15	16	17	18	19	20
21	22	23	24	25	26	27
28	29	30	31			

April

MON	TUE	WED	THU	FRI	SAT	SUN
				1	2	3
4	5	6	7	8	9	10
11	12	13	14	15	16	17
18	19	20	21	22	23	24
25	26	27	28	29	30	

May

MON	TUE	WED	THU	FRI	SAT	SUN
						1
2	3	4	5	6	7	8
9	10	11	12	13	14	15
16	17	18	19	20	21	22
23	24	25	26	27	28	29
30	31					

June

MON	TUE	WED	THU	FRI	SAT	SUN
		1	2	3	4	5
6	7	8	9	10	11	12
13	14	15	16	17	18	19
20	21	22	23	24	25	26
27	28	29	30			

Notes

2022

July

MON	TUE	WED	THU	FRI	SAT	SUN
				1	2	3
4	5	6	7	8	9	10
11	12	13	14	15	16	17
18	19	20	21	22	23	24
25	26	27	28	29	30	31

August

MON	TUE	WED	THU	FRI	SAT	SUN
1	2	3	4	5	6	7
8	9	10	11	12	13	14
15	16	17	18	19	20	21
22	23	24	25	26	27	28
29	30	31				

September

MON	TUE	WED	THU	FRI	SAT	SUN
			1	2	3	4
5	6	7	8	9	10	11
12	13	14	15	16	17	18
19	20	21	22	23	24	25
26	27	28	29	30		

October

MON	TUE	WED	THU	FRI	SAT	SUN
					1	2
3	4	5	6	7	8	9
10	11	12	13	14	15	16
17	18	19	20	21	22	23
24	25	26	27	28	29	30
31						

November

MON	TUE	WED	THU	FRI	SAT	SUN
	1	2	3	4	5	6
7	8	9	10	11	12	13
14	15	16	17	18	19	20
21	22	23	24	25	26	27
28	29	30				

December

MON	TUE	WED	THU	FRI	SAT	SUN
			1	2	3	4
5	6	7	8	9	10	11
12	13	14	15	16	17	18
19	20	21	22	23	24	25
26	27	28	29	30	31	

Notes

_____

_____

_____

_____

_____

_____

_____

_____

_____

_____

YEARLY PLANNER

2022

	January	February	March	April	May	June
1						
2						
3						
4						
5						
6						
7						
8						
9						
10						
11						
12						
13						
14						
15						
16						
17						
18						
19						
20						
21						
22						
23						
24						
25						
26						
27						
28						
29						
30						
31						

YEARLY PLANNER

2022

	July	August	September	October	November	December
1						
2						
3						
4						
5						
6						
7						
8						
9						
10						
11						
12						
13						
14						
15						
16						
17						
18						
19						
20						
21						
22						
23						
24						
25						
26						
27						
28						
29						
30						
31						

January

2022

MONDAY	TUESDAY	WEDNESDAY	THURSDAY
3	4	5	6
10	11	12	13
17	18	19	20
24	25	26	27
31			

anuary

2022

FRIDAY	SATURDAY	SUNDAY	NOTES
	1	2	_____
7	8	9	_____
14	15	16	_____
21	22	23	_____
28	29	30	_____

February

202

MONDAY	TUESDAY	WEDNESDAY	THURSDAY
		1	2
7	8	9	1
14	15	16	1
21	22	23	2
28			

ebruary 2022

FRIDAY	SATURDAY	SUNDAY	NOTES
4	5	6	_____
			_____
			_____
11	12	13	_____
			_____
			_____
18	19	20	_____
			_____
			_____
25	26	27	_____
			_____
			_____
			_____
			_____
			_____
			_____
			_____

March

2022

MONDAY	TUESDAY	WEDNESDAY	THURSDAY
	1	2	3
7	8	9	10
14	15	16	17
21	22	23	24
28	29	30	31

March 2022

FRIDAY	SATURDAY	SUNDAY	NOTES
4	5	6	
11	12	13	
18	19	20	
25	26	27	

April 2022

MONDAY	TUESDAY	WEDNESDAY	THURSDAY
4	5	6	7
11	12	13	14
18	19	20	21
25	26	27	28

April 2022

FRIDAY	SATURDAY	SUNDAY	NOTES
1	2	3	_____
			_____
			_____
8	9	10	_____
			_____
			_____
15	16	17	_____
			_____
			_____
22	23	24	_____
			_____
			_____
29	30		_____
			_____
			_____
			_____
			_____

May 2022

MONDAY	TUESDAY	WEDNESDAY	THURSDAY
2	3	4	5
9	10	11	12
16	17	18	19
23	24	25	26
30	31		

May

2022

FRIDAY	SATURDAY	SUNDAY	NOTES
		1	
6	7	8	
13	14	15	
20	21	22	
27	28	29	

June

2022

MONDAY	TUESDAY	WEDNESDAY	THURSDAY
		1	2
6	7	8	9
13	14	15	16
20	21	22	23
27	28	29	30

June

2022

FRIDAY	SATURDAY	SUNDAY	NOTES
3	4	5	_____
			_____
			_____
10	11	12	_____
			_____
			_____
17	18	19	_____
			_____
			_____
24	25	26	_____
			_____
			_____
			_____
			_____
			_____
			_____

July

2022

MONDAY	TUESDAY	WEDNESDAY	THURSDAY
4	5	6	7
11	12	13	14
18	19	20	21
25	26	27	28

July

2022

FRIDAY	SATURDAY	SUNDAY	NOTES
1	2	3	
8	9	10	
15	16	17	
22	23	24	
29	30	31	

August 2022

MONDAY	TUESDAY	WEDNESDAY	THURSDAY
1	2	3	4
8	9	10	11
15	16	17	18
22	23	24	25
29	30	31	

August

2022

FRIDAY	SATURDAY	SUNDAY	NOTES
5	6	7	
12	13	14	
19	20	21	
26	27	28	

September 2022

MONDAY	TUESDAY	WEDNESDAY	THURSDAY
			1
5	6	7	8
12	13	14	15
19	20	21	22
26	27	28	29

September

2022

FRIDAY	SATURDAY	SUNDAY	NOTES
3	4	5	
10	11	12	
17	18	19	
24	25	26	
30			

October

2022

MONDAY	TUESDAY	WEDNESDAY	THURSDAY
3	4	5	6
10	11	12	13
17	18	19	20
24	25	26	27
31			

October

2022

FRIDAY	SATURDAY	SUNDAY	NOTES
	1	2	_____
			_____
7	8	9	_____
			_____
14	15	16	_____
			_____
21	22	23	_____
			_____
28	29	30	_____
			_____
			_____
			_____

November 2022

MONDAY	TUESDAY	WEDNESDAY	THURSDAY
	1	2	3
7	8	9	10
14	15	16	17
21	22	23	24
28	29	30	

November 2022

FRIDAY	SATURDAY	SUNDAY	NOTES
4	5	6	
11	12	13	
18	19	20	
25	26	27	

December

202

MONDAY	TUESDAY	WEDNESDAY	THURSDAY
5	6	7	
12	13	14	1
19	20	21	2
26	27	28	2

December 2022

FRIDAY	SATURDAY	SUNDAY	NOTES
2	3	4	
9	10	11	
16	17	18	
23	24	25	
30	31		

List Name _____   Date _____

List Name _____   Date _____

List Name _____   *Date* _____

_____
_____
_____
_____
_____
_____
_____
_____
_____
_____
_____
_____
_____
_____
_____
_____
_____
_____
_____
_____
_____
_____
_____

List Name _____   *Date* _____

_____
_____
_____
_____
_____
_____
_____
_____
_____
_____
_____
_____
_____
_____
_____
_____
_____
_____
_____
_____
_____
_____
_____
_____
_____
_____
_____
_____
_____

List Name _____   *Date* _____

_____
_____
_____
_____
_____
_____
_____
_____
_____
_____
_____
_____
_____
_____
_____
_____
_____
_____
_____
_____
_____
_____

List Name _____   Date _____

List Name _____   *Date* _____

_____
_____
_____
_____
_____
_____
_____
_____
_____
_____
_____
_____
_____
_____
_____
_____
_____
_____
_____
_____
_____
_____
_____
_____

List Name _____   *Date* _____

_____

_____

_____

_____

_____

_____

_____

_____

_____

_____

_____

_____

_____

_____

_____

_____

_____

_____

_____

_____

_____

_____

_____

_____

_____

List Name _____   *Date* _____

_____

_____

_____

_____

_____

_____

_____

_____

_____

_____

_____

_____

_____

_____

_____

_____

_____

_____

_____

_____

_____

_____

_____

_____

st Name _____   Date _____

List Name _____ Date _____

First Name _____   Date _____

_____
_____
_____
_____
_____
_____
_____
_____
_____
_____
_____
_____
_____
_____
_____
_____
_____
_____
_____
_____
_____
_____
_____
_____

List Name _____   Date _____

ist Name _____   Date _____

List Name _____ *Date* _____

_____
_____
_____
_____
_____
_____
_____
_____
_____
_____
_____
_____
_____
_____
_____
_____
_____
_____
_____
_____
_____
_____

List Name _____   Date _____

_____
_____
_____
_____
_____
_____
_____
_____
_____
_____
_____
_____
_____
_____
_____
_____
_____
_____
_____
_____
_____
_____
_____
_____

List Name _____   *Date* _____

List Name _____ *Date* _____

_____
_____
_____
_____
_____
_____
_____
_____
_____
_____
_____
_____
_____
_____
_____
_____
_____
_____
_____
_____
_____
_____
_____
_____
_____
_____
_____
_____
_____

List Name _____   Date _____

List Name _____   Date _____

_____

_____

_____

_____

_____

_____

_____

_____

_____

_____

_____

_____

_____

_____

_____

_____

_____

_____

_____

_____

_____

_____

_____

_____

List Name _____ *Date* _____

_____
_____
_____
_____
_____
_____
_____
_____
_____
_____
_____
_____
_____
_____
_____
_____
_____
_____
_____
_____
_____
_____
_____
_____

List Name _____   Date _____

List Name _____   Date _____

List Name _____   *Date* _____

_____
_____
_____
_____
_____
_____
_____
_____
_____
_____
_____
_____
_____
_____
_____
_____
_____
_____
_____
_____
_____
_____
_____

List Name _____   *Date* _____

_____

_____

_____

_____

_____

_____

_____

_____

_____

_____

_____

_____

_____

_____

_____

_____

_____

_____

_____

_____

_____

_____

List Name _____   *Date* _____

List Name _____ Date _____

List Name _____   Date _____

List Name _____ Date _____

List Name _____   Date _____

List Name _____   *Date* _____

_____

_____

_____

_____

_____

_____

_____

_____

_____

_____

_____

_____

_____

_____

_____

_____

_____

_____

_____

_____

_____

List Name _____   Date _____

List Name _____   Date _____

_____
_____
_____
_____
_____
_____
_____
_____
_____
_____
_____
_____
_____
_____
_____
_____
_____
_____
_____
_____
_____
_____
_____

ist Name _____   Date _____

List Name _____   *Date* _____

st Name _____   Date _____

List Name _____   Date _____

List Name _____   Date _____

_____

_____

_____

_____

_____

_____

_____

_____

_____

_____

_____

_____

_____

_____

_____

_____

_____

_____

_____

_____

_____

_____

_____

_____

_____

_____

_____

_____

List Name _____   *Date* _____

_____

_____

_____

_____

_____

_____

_____

_____

_____

_____

_____

_____

_____

_____

_____

_____

_____

_____

_____

_____

_____

List Name _____   Date _____

_____
_____
_____
_____
_____
_____
_____
_____
_____
_____
_____
_____
_____
_____
_____
_____
_____
_____
_____
_____
_____
_____
_____
_____
_____
_____

List Name _____   *Date* _____

List Name _____   Date _____

List Name _____   *Date* _____

_____
_____
_____
_____
_____
_____
_____
_____
_____
_____
_____
_____
_____
_____
_____
_____
_____
_____
_____
_____
_____
_____
_____
_____
_____

List Name _____   *Date* _____

List Name _____   Date _____

List Name _____   Date _____

_____
_____
_____
_____
_____
_____
_____
_____
_____
_____
_____
_____
_____
_____
_____
_____
_____
_____
_____
_____
_____
_____
_____
_____
_____
_____
_____
_____

List Name _____   *Date* _____

List Name _____   Date _____

_____
_____
_____
_____
_____
_____
_____
_____
_____
_____
_____
_____
_____
_____
_____
_____
_____
_____
_____
_____
_____
_____
_____
_____
_____
_____
_____

List Name _____   *Date* _____

List Name _____ Date _____

List Name _____   *Date* _____

List Name _____   Date _____

List Name _____   *Date* _____

_____
_____
_____
_____
_____
_____
_____
_____
_____
_____
_____
_____
_____
_____
_____
_____
_____
_____
_____
_____
_____
_____
_____

List Name _____   Date _____

List Name _____   *Date* _____

_____

_____

_____

_____

_____

_____

_____

_____

_____

_____

_____

_____

_____

_____

_____

_____

_____

_____

_____

_____

List Name _____ *Date* _____

_____
_____
_____
_____
_____
_____
_____
_____
_____
_____
_____
_____
_____
_____
_____
_____
_____
_____
_____
_____
_____
_____
_____

List Name _____   Date _____

List Name _____   Date _____

List Name _____   *Date* _____

_____
_____
_____
_____
_____
_____
_____
_____
_____
_____
_____
_____
_____
_____
_____
_____
_____
_____
_____
_____
_____
_____
_____
_____

List Name _____   *Date* _____

My Plant Log 🍃🍂

Plant Name: _____

Date Planted: _____

Purchased At: _____

Price: _____

☐ Seed ☐ Planting ☐ Cutting ☐ Bulb

Water: 💧 💧💧 💧💧💧   **Sunlight:** ☀ 🌤 ⬤

Date	Plant History
_____	_____
_____	_____
_____	_____
_____	_____
_____	_____
_____	_____

Notes

My Plant Log 🌿🍃

Plant Name: _____

Date Planted: _____

Purchased At: _____

Price: _____

☐ Seed ☐ Planting ☐ Cutting ☐ Bulb

Water: 💧 💧💧 💧💧💧   **Sunlight:** ☀ ◐ ●

Date	Plant History
_____	_____
_____	_____
_____	_____
_____	_____
_____	_____
_____	_____

Notes

My Plant Log 🍃🍂

Plant Name: _____

Date Planted: _____

Purchased At: _____

Price: _____

☐ Seed ☐ Planting ☐ Cutting ☐ Bulb

Water: 💧 💧💧 💧💧💧   **Sunlight:** ☀ ◑ ●

Date	Plant History
_____	_____
_____	_____
_____	_____
_____	_____
_____	_____
_____	_____

Notes

My Plant Log

Plant Name: _____

Date Planted: _____

Purchased At: _____

Price: _____

☐ Seed ☐ Planting ☐ Cutting ☐ Bulb

Water: 💧 💧💧 💧💧💧   Sunlight: ☀ ☽ ●

Date	Plant History
_____	_____
_____	_____
_____	_____
_____	_____
_____	_____
_____	_____

Notes

My Plant Log 🍃🍃

Plant Name: _____

Date Planted: _____

Purchased At: _____

Price: _____

☐ Seed ☐ Planting ☐ Cutting ☐ Bulb

Water: 💧 💧💧 💧💧💧   **Sunlight:** ☀ ☀ ⬤

Date	Plant History
_____	_____
_____	_____
_____	_____
_____	_____
_____	_____
_____	_____

Notes

My Plant Log

Plant Name: _____

Date Planted: _____

Purchased At: _____

Price: _____

☐ Seed ☐ Planting ☐ Cutting ☐ Bulb

Water: 💧 💧💧 💧💧💧   **Sunlight:** ☀ ☀ ⬤

Date	Plant History
_____	_____
_____	_____
_____	_____
_____	_____
_____	_____
_____	_____

Notes

My Plant Log 🍃🍂

Plant Name: _____

Date Planted: _____

Purchased At: _____

Price: _____

☐ Seed ☐ Planting ☐ Cutting ☐ Bulb

Water: 💧 💧💧 💧💧💧   **Sunlight:** ☀ 🌤 ⬤

Date	Plant History
_____	_____
_____	_____
_____	_____
_____	_____
_____	_____
_____	_____

Notes

My Plant Log

Plant Name: _____

Date Planted: _____

Purchased At: _____

Price: _____

☐ Seed ☐ Planting ☐ Cutting ☐ Bulb

Water: 💧 💧💧 💧💧💧   **Sunlight:** ☀ ☀ ⬤

Date	Plant History
_____	_____
_____	_____
_____	_____
_____	_____
_____	_____
_____	_____

Notes

My Plant Log 🍃🍃

Plant Name: _____

Date Planted: _____

Purchased At: _____

Price: _____

☐ Seed ☐ Planting ☐ Cutting ☐ Bulb

Water: 💧 💧💧 💧💧💧 💧   **Sunlight:** ☀ 🌤 ⚫

Date	Plant History
_____	_____
_____	_____
_____	_____
_____	_____
_____	_____

Notes

My Plant Log 🌿🍃

Plant Name: _____

Date Planted: _____

Purchased At: _____

Price: _____

☐ Seed ☐ Planting ☐ Cutting ☐ Bulb

Water: 💧 💧💧 💧💧💧   **Sunlight:** ☀ ◐ ●

Date	Plant History
_____	_____
_____	_____
_____	_____
_____	_____
_____	_____
_____	_____

Notes

My Plant Log 🍃🍃

Plant Name: _____

Date Planted: _____

Purchased At: _____

Price: _____

☐ Seed ☐ Planting ☐ Cutting ☐ Bulb

Water: 💧 💧💧 💧💧💧   **Sunlight:** ☀ ◐ ●

Date	Plant History
_____	_____
_____	_____
_____	_____
_____	_____
_____	_____
_____	_____

Notes

My Plant Log

Plant Name: _____

Date Planted: _____

Purchased At: _____

Price: _____

☐ Seed ☐ Planting ☐ Cutting ☐ Bulb

Water: 🌢 🌢🌢 🌢🌢🌢   **Sunlight:** ☀ ☀ ●

Date	Plant History
_____	_____
_____	_____
_____	_____
_____	_____
_____	_____
_____	_____

Notes

My Plant Log

Plant Name: _____

Date Planted: _____

Purchased At: _____

Price: _____

☐ Seed   ☐ Planting   ☐ Cutting   ☐ Bulb

Water: 💧 💧💧 💧💧💧   **Sunlight:** ☀ 🌤 ⬤

Date	Plant History
_____	_____
_____	_____
_____	_____
_____	_____
_____	_____
_____	_____

Notes

My Plant Log

Plant Name: _____

Date Planted: _____

Purchased At: _____

Price: _____

☐ Seed ☐ Planting ☐ Cutting ☐ Bulb

Water: 💧 💧💧 💧💧💧   **Sunlight:** ☀ ◑ ●

Date	Plant History
_____	_____
_____	_____
_____	_____
_____	_____
_____	_____

Notes

My Plant Log 🌿🍃

Plant Name: _____

Date Planted: _____

Purchased At: _____

Price: _____

☐ Seed ☐ Planting ☐ Cutting ☐ Bulb

Water: 💧 💧💧 💧💧💧   Sunlight: ☀ 🌤 🌑

Date	Plant History
_____	_____
_____	_____
_____	_____
_____	_____
_____	_____

Notes

My Plant Log

Plant Name: _____

Date Planted: _____

Purchased At: _____

Price: _____

☐ Seed ☐ Planting ☐ Cutting ☐ Bulb

Water: 💧 💧💧 💧💧💧   **Sunlight:** ☀ 🌤 ⬤

Date	Plant History
_____	_____
_____	_____
_____	_____
_____	_____
_____	_____
_____	_____

Notes

My Plant Log

Plant Name: _____

Date Planted: _____

Purchased At: _____

Price: _____

☐ Seed   ☐ Planting   ☐ Cutting   ☐ Bulb

Water: 💧 💧💧 💧💧💧   **Sunlight:** ☀ ☀ ●

Date	Plant History
_____	_____
_____	_____
_____	_____
_____	_____
_____	_____
_____	_____

Notes

My Plant Log 🍃🍂

Plant Name: _____

Date Planted: _____

Purchased At: _____

Price: _____

☐ Seed ☐ Planting ☐ Cutting ☐ Bulb

Water: 💧 💧💧 💧💧💧   **Sunlight:** ☀ 🌤 ⚫

Date	Plant History
_____	_____
_____	_____
_____	_____
_____	_____
_____	_____
_____	_____

Notes

My Plant Log 🍃🍂

Plant Name: _____

Date Planted: _____

Purchased At: _____

Price: _____

☐ Seed   ☐ Planting   ☐ Cutting   ☐ Bulb

Water: 💧 💧💧 💧💧💧   **Sunlight:** ☀ ◑ ●

Date	Plant History
_____	_____
_____	_____
_____	_____
_____	_____
_____	_____
_____	_____

Notes

My Plant Log 🍃🍃

Plant Name: _____

Date Planted: _____

Purchased At: _____

Price: _____

☐ Seed   ☐ Planting   ☐ Cutting   ☐ Bulb

Water: 💧 💧💧 💧💧💧   **Sunlight:** ☀ ☽ ●

Date	Plant History
_____	_____
_____	_____
_____	_____
_____	_____
_____	_____
_____	_____

Notes

My Plant Log

Plant Name: _____

Date Planted: _____

Purchased At: _____

Price: _____

☐ Seed ☐ Planting ☐ Cutting ☐ Bulb

Water: 💧 💧💧 💧💧💧   **Sunlight:** ☀ ☼ ●

Date	Plant History
_____	_____
_____	_____
_____	_____
_____	_____
_____	_____
_____	_____

Notes

My Plant Log 🍃🍃

Plant Name: _____

Date Planted: _____

Purchased At: _____

Price: _____

☐ Seed ☐ Planting ☐ Cutting ☐ Bulb

Water: 💧 💧💧 💧💧💧   **Sunlight:** ☀️ 🌤️ ●

Date	Plant History
_____	_____
_____	_____
_____	_____
_____	_____
_____	_____
_____	_____

Notes

My Plant Log

Plant Name: _____

Date Planted: _____

Purchased At: _____

Price: _____

☐ Seed ☐ Planting ☐ Cutting ☐ Bulb

Water: 💧 💧💧 💧💧💧   **Sunlight:** ☀ 🌤 ●

Date	Plant History
_____	_____
_____	_____
_____	_____
_____	_____
_____	_____
_____	_____

Notes

My Plant Log 🌿🍃

Plant Name: _____

Date Planted: _____

Purchased At: _____

Price: _____

☐ Seed ☐ Planting ☐ Cutting ☐ Bulb

Water: 💧 💧💧 💧💧💧   **Sunlight:** ☀ 🌤 ⬤

Date	Plant History
_____	_____
_____	_____
_____	_____
_____	_____
_____	_____
_____	_____

Notes

My Plant Log 🌿🍃

Plant Name: _____

Date Planted: _____

Purchased At: _____

Price: _____

☐ Seed ☐ Planting ☐ Cutting ☐ Bulb

Water: 💧 💧💧 💧💧💧   **Sunlight:** ☀ ☀ ●

Date	Plant History
_____	_____
_____	_____
_____	_____
_____	_____
_____	_____
_____	_____

Notes

My Plant Log 🌿🍃

Plant Name: _____

Date Planted: _____

Purchased At: _____

Price: _____

☐ Seed ☐ Planting ☐ Cutting ☐ Bulb

Water: 💧 💧💧 💧💧💧   **Sunlight:** ☀ 🌤 ●

Date	Plant History
_____	_____
_____	_____
_____	_____
_____	_____
_____	_____
_____	_____

Notes

My Plant Log 🍃🍃

Plant Name: _____

Date Planted: _____

Purchased At: _____

Price: _____

☐ Seed   ☐ Planting   ☐ Cutting   ☐ Bulb

Water: 💧 💧💧 💧💧💧   **Sunlight:** ☀ ☼ ●

Date	Plant History
_____	_____
_____	_____
_____	_____
_____	_____
_____	_____
_____	_____

Notes

My Plant Log 🍃🍂

Plant Name: _____

Date Planted: _____

Purchased At: _____

Price: _____

☐ Seed ☐ Planting ☐ Cutting ☐ Bulb

Water: 💧 💧💧 💧💧💧   Sunlight: ☀️ 🌤️ ⚫

Date	Plant History
_____	_____
_____	_____
_____	_____
_____	_____
_____	_____

Notes

My Plant Log 🍃🍂

Plant Name: _____

Date Planted: _____

Purchased At: _____

Price: _____

☐ Seed   ☐ Planting   ☐ Cutting   ☐ Bulb

Water: 💧 💧💧 💧💧💧   **Sunlight:** ☀ ◐ ●

Date	Plant History
_____	_____
_____	_____
_____	_____
_____	_____
_____	_____

Notes

My Plant Log 🌿🍃

Plant Name: _____

Date Planted: _____

Purchased At: _____

Price: _____

☐ Seed ☐ Planting ☐ Cutting ☐ Bulb

Water: 💧 💧💧 💧💧💧   **Sunlight:** ☀ ☀ ●

Date	Plant History
_____	_____
_____	_____
_____	_____
_____	_____
_____	_____
_____	_____

Notes

My Plant Log

Plant Name: _____

Date Planted: _____

Purchased At: _____

Price: _____

☐ Seed ☐ Planting ☐ Cutting ☐ Bulb

Water: 💧 💧💧 💧💧💧   Sunlight: ☀ 🌤 ⬤

Date	Plant History
_____	_____
_____	_____
_____	_____
_____	_____
_____	_____

Notes

My Plant Log

Plant Name: _____

Date Planted: _____

Purchased At: _____

Price: _____

☐ Seed ☐ Planting ☐ Cutting ☐ Bulb

Water: 💧 💧💧 💧💧💧   Sunlight: ☀ ☀ ●

Date	Plant History
_____	_____
_____	_____
_____	_____
_____	_____
_____	_____
_____	_____

Notes

My Plant Log

Plant Name: _____

Date Planted: _____

Purchased At: _____

Price: _____

☐ Seed   ☐ Planting   ☐ Cutting   ☐ Bulb

Water: 🌢 🌢🌢 🌢🌢🌢   **Sunlight:** ☀ ◐ ●

Date	Plant History
_____	_____
_____	_____
_____	_____
_____	_____
_____	_____
_____	_____

Notes

My Plant Log

Plant Name: _____

Date Planted: _____

Purchased At: _____

Price: _____

☐ Seed ☐ Planting ☐ Cutting ☐ Bulb

Water: 💧 💧💧 💧💧💧   Sunlight: ☼ ◐ ●

Date	Plant History
_____	_____
_____	_____
_____	_____
_____	_____
_____	_____
_____	_____

Notes

My Plant Log

Plant Name: _____

Date Planted: _____

Purchased At: _____

Price: _____

☐ Seed ☐ Planting ☐ Cutting ☐ Bulb

Water: 💧 💧💧 💧💧💧 💧   Sunlight: ☀ ☀ ●

Date	Plant History
_____	_____
_____	_____
_____	_____
_____	_____
_____	_____
_____	_____

Notes

My Plant Log

Plant Name: _____

Date Planted: _____

Purchased At: _____

Price: _____

☐ Seed ☐ Planting ☐ Cutting ☐ Bulb

Water: 💧 💧💧 💧💧💧 **Sunlight:** ☀ ☼ ●

Date	Plant History
_____	_____
_____	_____
_____	_____
_____	_____
_____	_____
_____	_____

Notes

My Plant Log 🌿🍃

Plant Name: _____

Date Planted: _____

Purchased At: _____

Price: _____

☐ Seed ☐ Planting ☐ Cutting ☐ Bulb

Water: 💧 💧💧 💧💧💧   **Sunlight:** ☀ 🌤 ⚫

Date	Plant History
_____	_____
_____	_____
_____	_____
_____	_____
_____	_____
_____	_____

Notes

My Plant Log 🍃🍃

Plant Name: _____

Date Planted: _____

Purchased At: _____

Price: _____

☐ Seed ☐ Planting ☐ Cutting ☐ Bulb

Water: 💧 💧💧 💧💧💧   **Sunlight:** ☀ ☽ ●

Date	Plant History
_____	_____
_____	_____
_____	_____
_____	_____
_____	_____
_____	_____

Notes

My Plant Log

Plant Name: _____

Date Planted: _____

Purchased At: _____

Price: _____

☐ Seed ☐ Planting ☐ Cutting ☐ Bulb

Water: 💧 💧💧 💧💧💧   **Sunlight:** ☀ ☀ ⬤

Date	Plant History
_____	_____
_____	_____
_____	_____
_____	_____
_____	_____
_____	_____

Notes

My Plant Log 🍃🍂

Plant Name: _____

Date Planted: _____

Purchased At: _____

Price: _____

☐ **Seed**   ☐ **Planting**   ☐ **Cutting**   ☐ **Bulb**

Water: 💧 💧💧 💧💧💧   **Sunlight:** ☀ ☀ ●

Date	Plant History
_____	_____
_____	_____
_____	_____
_____	_____
_____	_____
_____	_____

Notes

My Plant Log 🍃🍂

Plant Name: _____

Date Planted: _____

Purchased At: _____

Price: _____

☐ Seed ☐ Planting ☐ Cutting ☐ Bulb

Water: 💧 💧💧 💧💧💧   **Sunlight:** ☀ ◑ ●

Date	Plant History
_____	_____
_____	_____
_____	_____
_____	_____
_____	_____
_____	_____

Notes

My Plant Log

Plant Name: _____

Date Planted: _____

Purchased At: _____

Price: _____

☐ Seed ☐ Planting ☐ Cutting ☐ Bulb

Water: 💧 💧💧 💧💧💧   **Sunlight:** ☀ 🌤 ⬤

Date	Plant History
_____	_____
_____	_____
_____	_____
_____	_____
_____	_____
_____	_____

Notes

My Plant Log 🍃🍃

Plant Name: _____

Date Planted: _____

Purchased At: _____

Price: _____

☐ Seed ☐ Planting ☐ Cutting ☐ Bulb

Water: 💧 💧💧 💧💧💧   **Sunlight:** ☀ ◑ ●

Date	Plant History
_____	_____
_____	_____
_____	_____
_____	_____
_____	_____
_____	_____

Notes

My Plant Log

Plant Name: _____

Date Planted: _____

Purchased At: _____

Price: _____

☐ Seed ☐ Planting ☐ Cutting ☐ Bulb

Water: 💧 💧💧 💧💧💧   **Sunlight:** ☀ ◑ ●

Date	Plant History
_____	_____
_____	_____
_____	_____
_____	_____
_____	_____
_____	_____

Notes

My Plant Log 🍃🍂

Plant Name: _____

Date Planted: _____

Purchased At: _____

Price: _____

☐ Seed ☐ Planting ☐ Cutting ☐ Bulb

Water: 💧 💧💧 💧💧💧   **Sunlight:** ☀ ◑ ●

Date	Plant History
_____	_____
_____	_____
_____	_____
_____	_____
_____	_____
_____	_____

Notes

My Plant Log

Plant Name: _____

Date Planted: _____

Purchased At: _____

Price: _____

☐ Seed ☐ Planting ☐ Cutting ☐ Bulb

Water: 🌢 🌢🌢 🌢🌢🌢   **Sunlight:** ☀ ☽ ●

Date	Plant History
_____	_____
_____	_____
_____	_____
_____	_____
_____	_____
_____	_____

Notes

My Plant Log

Plant Name: _____

Date Planted: _____

Purchased At: _____

Price: _____

☐ Seed ☐ Planting ☐ Cutting ☐ Bulb

Water: 💧 💧💧 💧💧💧   **Sunlight:** ☀ ◑ ●

Date	Plant History
_____	_____
_____	_____
_____	_____
_____	_____
_____	_____
_____	_____

Notes

My Plant Log

Plant Name: _____

Date Planted: _____

Purchased At: _____

Price: _____

☐ Seed ☐ Planting ☐ Cutting ☐ Bulb

Water: 💧 💧💧 💧💧💧 **Sunlight:** ☀ 🌤 ⚫

Date	Plant History
_____	_____
_____	_____
_____	_____
_____	_____
_____	_____
_____	_____

Notes

My Plant Log

Plant Name: _____

Date Planted: _____

Purchased At: _____

Price: _____

☐ Seed ☐ Planting ☐ Cutting ☐ Bulb

Water: 💧 💧💧 💧💧💧   **Sunlight:** ☀ 🌤 ⬤

Date	Plant History
_____	_____
_____	_____
_____	_____
_____	_____
_____	_____
_____	_____

Notes

My Plant Log 🍃🍃

Plant Name: _____

Date Planted: _____

Purchased At: _____

Price: _____

☐ Seed ☐ Planting ☐ Cutting ☐ Bulb

Water: 💧 💧💧 💧💧💧   **Sunlight:** ☀ 🌤 ⚫

Date	Plant History
_____	_____
_____	_____
_____	_____
_____	_____
_____	_____
_____	_____

Notes

My Plant Log

Plant Name: _____

Date Planted: _____

Purchased At: _____

Price: _____

☐ Seed ☐ Planting ☐ Cutting ☐ Bulb

Water: 💧 💧💧 💧💧💧   Sunlight: ☼ ☀ ●

Date	Plant History
_____	_____
_____	_____
_____	_____
_____	_____
_____	_____
_____	_____

Notes

My Plant Log

Plant Name: _____

Date Planted: _____

Purchased At: _____

Price: _____

☐ Seed ☐ Planting ☐ Cutting ☐ Bulb

Water: 💧 💧💧 💧💧💧   **Sunlight:** ☼ ☽ ●

Date	Plant History
_____	_____
_____	_____
_____	_____
_____	_____
_____	_____
_____	_____

Notes

My Plant Log

Plant Name: _____

Date Planted: _____

Purchased At: _____

Price: _____

☐ Seed ☐ Planting ☐ Cutting ☐ Bulb

Water: 💧 💧💧 💧💧💧   **Sunlight:** ☀ 🌤 ⚫

Date	Plant History
_____	_____
_____	_____
_____	_____
_____	_____
_____	_____
_____	_____

Notes

My Plant Log 🍃🍃

Plant Name: _____

Date Planted: _____

Purchased At: _____

Price: _____

☐ Seed ☐ Planting ☐ Cutting ☐ Bulb

Water: 💧 💧💧 💧💧💧   Sunlight: ☀ 🌤 ⚫

Date	Plant History
_____	_____
_____	_____
_____	_____
_____	_____
_____	_____
_____	_____

Notes

My Plant Log

Plant Name: _____

Date Planted: _____

Purchased At: _____

Price: _____

☐ Seed ☐ Planting ☐ Cutting ☐ Bulb

Water: 💧 💧💧 💧💧💧   **Sunlight:** ☀ 🌤 ⬤

Date	Plant History
_____	_____
_____	_____
_____	_____
_____	_____
_____	_____
_____	_____

Notes

My Plant Log 🌿🍃

Plant Name: _____

Date Planted: _____

Purchased At: _____

Price: _____

☐ Seed ☐ Planting ☐ Cutting ☐ Bulb

Water: 💧 💧💧 💧💧💧 **Sunlight:** ☀ ☀ ⬤

Date	Plant History
_____	_____
_____	_____
_____	_____
_____	_____
_____	_____
_____	_____

Notes

My Plant Log

Plant Name: _____

Date Planted: _____

Purchased At: _____

Price: _____

☐ Seed ☐ Planting ☐ Cutting ☐ Bulb

Water: 💧 💧💧 💧💧💧   **Sunlight:** ☀ ☀ ⚫

Date	Plant History
_____	_____
_____	_____
_____	_____
_____	_____
_____	_____
_____	_____

Notes

My Plant Log 🍃🍃

Plant Name: _____

Date Planted: _____

Purchased At: _____

Price: _____

☐ Seed   ☐ Planting   ☐ Cutting   ☐ Bulb

Water: 💧 💧💧 💧💧💧   **Sunlight:** ☀ 🌤 ●

Date	Plant History
_____	_____
_____	_____
_____	_____
_____	_____
_____	_____
_____	_____

Notes

My Plant Log 🍃🍂

Plant Name: _____

Date Planted: _____

Purchased At: _____

Price: _____

☐ Seed   ☐ Planting   ☐ Cutting   ☐ Bulb

Water: 💧 💧💧 💧💧💧   **Sunlight:** ☀ 🌤 ⚫

Date	Plant History
_____	_____
_____	_____
_____	_____
_____	_____
_____	_____
_____	_____

Notes

My Plant Log 🍃🍃

Plant Name: _____

Date Planted: _____

Purchased At: _____

Price: _____

☐ Seed ☐ Planting ☐ Cutting ☐ Bulb

Water: 💧 💧💧 💧💧💧   **Sunlight:** ☀ 🌤 ●

Date	Plant History
_____	_____
_____	_____
_____	_____
_____	_____
_____	_____
_____	_____

Notes

My Plant Log

Plant Name: _____

Date Planted: _____

Purchased At: _____

Price: _____

☐ Seed ☐ Planting ☐ Cutting ☐ Bulb

Water: 🌢 🌢🌢 🌢🌢🌢   **Sunlight:** ☀ ☼ ●

Date	Plant History
_____	_____
_____	_____
_____	_____
_____	_____
_____	_____
_____	_____

Notes

My Plant Log 🍃🍂

Plant Name: _____

Date Planted: _____

Purchased At: _____

Price: _____

☐ Seed ☐ Planting ☐ Cutting ☐ Bulb

Water: 💧 💧💧 💧💧💧   **Sunlight:** ☀ 🌤 ⚫

Date	Plant History
_____	_____
_____	_____
_____	_____
_____	_____
_____	_____
_____	_____

Notes

My Plant Log 🍃🍂

Plant Name: _____

Date Planted: _____

Purchased At: _____

Price: _____

☐ Seed ☐ Planting ☐ Cutting ☐ Bulb

Water: 💧 💧💧 💧💧💧   **Sunlight:** ☀ ☼ ⬤

Date	Plant History
_____	_____
_____	_____
_____	_____
_____	_____
_____	_____
_____	_____

Notes

My Plant Log 🍃

Plant Name: _____

Date Planted: _____

Purchased At: _____

Price: _____

☐ Seed ☐ Planting ☐ Cutting ☐ Bulb

Water: 💧 💧💧 💧💧💧   **Sunlight:** ☀ 🌤 ⚫

Date	Plant History
_____	_____
_____	_____
_____	_____
_____	_____
_____	_____
_____	_____

Notes

My Plant Log

Plant Name: _____

Date Planted: _____

Purchased At: _____

Price: _____

☐ Seed ☐ Planting ☐ Cutting ☐ Bulb

Water: 💧 💧💧 💧💧💧   Sunlight: ☀ ◑ ●

Date	Plant History
_____	_____
_____	_____
_____	_____
_____	_____
_____	_____
_____	_____

Notes

My Plant Log

Plant Name: _____

Date Planted: _____

Purchased At: _____

Price: _____

☐ Seed ☐ Planting ☐ Cutting ☐ Bulb

Water: 💧 💧💧 💧💧💧   Sunlight: ☀ 🌓 ⚫

Date	Plant History
_____	_____
_____	_____
_____	_____
_____	_____
_____	_____
_____	_____

Notes

My Plant Log

Plant Name: _____

Date Planted: _____

Purchased At: _____

Price: _____

☐ Seed ☐ Planting ☐ Cutting ☐ Bulb

Water: 🌢 🌢🌢 🌢🌢🌢   **Sunlight:** ☀ ◐ ●

Date	Plant History
_____	_____
_____	_____
_____	_____
_____	_____
_____	_____

Notes

My Plant Log 🍃🍂

Plant Name: _____

Date Planted: _____

Purchased At: _____

Price: _____

☐ Seed ☐ Planting ☐ Cutting ☐ Bulb

Water: 💧 💧💧 💧💧💧   **Sunlight:** ☀ 🌤 ⬤

Date	Plant History
_____	_____
_____	_____
_____	_____
_____	_____
_____	_____
_____	_____

Notes

My Plant Log 🍃🍂

Plant Name: _____

Date Planted: _____

Purchased At: _____

Price: _____

☐ Seed ☐ Planting ☐ Cutting ☐ Bulb

Water: 💧 💧💧 💧💧💧   **Sunlight:** ☀ ◐ ●

Date	Plant History
_____	_____
_____	_____
_____	_____
_____	_____
_____	_____

Notes

My Plant Log 🍃🍂

Plant Name: _____

Date Planted: _____

Purchased At: _____

Price: _____

☐ Seed ☐ Planting ☐ Cutting ☐ Bulb

Water: 💧 💧💧 💧💧💧   **Sunlight:** ☀ ◐ ●

Date	Plant History
_____	_____
_____	_____
_____	_____
_____	_____
_____	_____

Notes

My Plant Log

Plant Name: _____

Date Planted: _____

Purchased At: _____

Price: _____

☐ Seed ☐ Planting ☐ Cutting ☐ Bulb

Water: 💧 💧💧 💧💧💧   **Sunlight:** ☀ ◐ ●

Date	Plant History
_____	_____
_____	_____
_____	_____
_____	_____
_____	_____
_____	_____

Notes

My Plant Log

Plant Name: _____

Date Planted: _____

Purchased At: _____

Price: _____

☐ Seed ☐ Planting ☐ Cutting ☐ Bulb

Water: 💧 💧💧 💧💧💧   **Sunlight:** ☀ ☀ ●

Date	Plant History
_____	_____
_____	_____
_____	_____
_____	_____
_____	_____
_____	_____

Notes

My Plant Log

Plant Name: _____

Date Planted: _____

Purchased At: _____

Price: _____

☐ Seed ☐ Planting ☐ Cutting ☐ Bulb

Water: 💧 💧💧 💧💧💧   **Sunlight:** ☀ ☀ ⬤

Date	Plant History
_____	_____
_____	_____
_____	_____
_____	_____
_____	_____
_____	_____

Notes

My Plant Log 🌿🍃

Plant Name: _____

Date Planted: _____

Purchased At: _____

Price: _____

☐ Seed ☐ Planting ☐ Cutting ☐ Bulb

Water: 💧 💧💧 💧💧💧 💧   **Sunlight:** ☼ ☽ ●

Date	Plant History
_____	_____
_____	_____
_____	_____
_____	_____
_____	_____
_____	_____

Notes

My Plant Log

Plant Name: _____

Date Planted: _____

Purchased At: _____

Price: _____

☐ Seed   ☐ Planting   ☐ Cutting   ☐ Bulb

Water: 💧 💧💧 💧💧💧   **Sunlight:** ☀ ◐ ●

Date	Plant History
_____	_____
_____	_____
_____	_____
_____	_____
_____	_____
_____	_____

Notes

My Plant Log

Plant Name: _____

Date Planted: _____

Purchased At: _____

Price: _____

☐ Seed   ☐ Planting   ☐ Cutting   ☐ Bulb

Water: 💧 💧💧 💧💧💧   Sunlight: ☀ ◑ ●

Date	Plant History
_____	_____
_____	_____
_____	_____
_____	_____
_____	_____
_____	_____

Notes

🌿🍃 Summary 🍃🍃

_____

_____

_____

_____

_____

_____

_____

_____

_____

_____

_____

_____

_____

_____

_____

_____

_____

_____

_____

_____

Summary

🍃🍃 Summary 🍃🍃

_____

_____

_____

_____

_____

_____

_____

_____

_____

_____

_____

_____

_____

_____

_____

_____

_____

_____

_____

_____

_____

Made in the USA
Middletown, DE
05 May 2022

65316020R00102